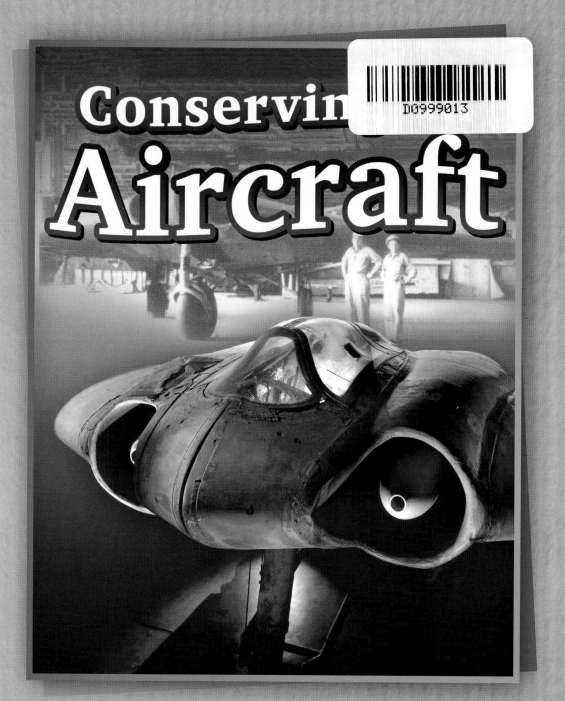

Conserving Aircraft

Ben Nussbaum

✳ Smithsonian

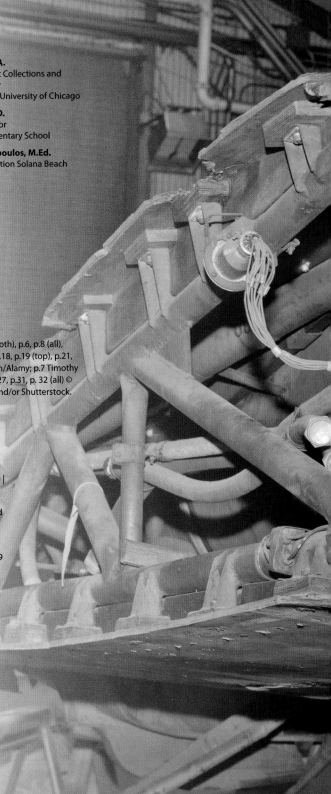

Contributing Author

Heather Schultz, M.A.

Consultants

Russell Lee
Chair, Department of Aeronautics
National Air and Space Museum

Lauren Horelick, M.A.
Objects Conservator, Smithsonian
National Air and Space Museum

Pete McElhinney
University of Bradford, UK

Anna Weiss-Pfau, M.A.
Campus and Public Art Collections and
Conservation Manager
Smart Museum of Art, University of Chicago

Tamieka Grizzle, Ed.D.
K–5 STEM Lab Instructor
Harmony Leland Elementary School

Stephanie Anastasopoulos, M.Ed.
TOSA, STREAM Integration Solana Beach
School District

Publishing Credits

Rachelle Cracchiolo, M.S.Ed., *Publisher*

Conni Medina, M.A.Ed., *Managing Editor*

Diana Kenney, M.A.Ed., NBCT, *Series Developer*

June Kikuchi, *Content Director*

Véronique Bos, *Creative Director*

Robin Erickson, *Art Director*

Seth Rogers, *Editor*

Mindy Duits, *Senior Graphic Designer*

Smithsonian Science Education Center

Image Credits: front cover, p.1 (both); back cover; pp.2–3, p.5 (both), p.6, p.8 (all), p.10, p.11 (both), p.12, p.13 (top), p.14 (both), p.15, p.17 (both), p.18, p.19 (top), p.21, p.22 (all), p.23, p.24, p.25 (top) © Smithsonian; p.4 David Coleman/Alamy; p.7 Timothy J. Bradley; p.16 (right) Dr. Keith Wheeler/Science Source; p.26, p.27, p.31, p. 32 (all) © Smithsonian, photo by Ben Nussbaum; all other images iStock and/or Shutterstock.

Library of Congress Cataloging-in-Publication Data

Names: Nussbaum, Ben, 1975- author.
Title: Conserving an aircraft / Ben Nussbaum.
Description: Huntington Beach, CA : Teacher Created Materials, [2019] | Audience: Grades 4-6. | Includes index. |
Identifiers: LCCN 2018005250 (print) | LCCN 2018010236 (ebook) | ISBN
  9781493869367 (E-book) | ISBN 9781493866960 (pbk.)
Subjects: LCSH: Horten 229 (Jet fighter plane)--Conservation and
  restoration--Juvenile literature. | Research aircraft--Germany--Juvenile
  literature. | Airplanes, Tailless--Germany--Juvenile literature.
Classification: LCC UG1242.F5 (ebook) | LCC UG1242.F5 N87 2019 (print) | DDC
  623.74/6340288--dc23
LC record available at https://lccn.loc.gov/2018005250

☼ Smithsonian

Teacher Created Materials

5301 Oceanus Drive
Huntington Beach, CA 92649-1030
www.tcmpub.com
ISBN 978-1-4938-6696-0
©2019 Teacher Created Materials, Inc.
Printed in China
Nordica.072018.CA21800844

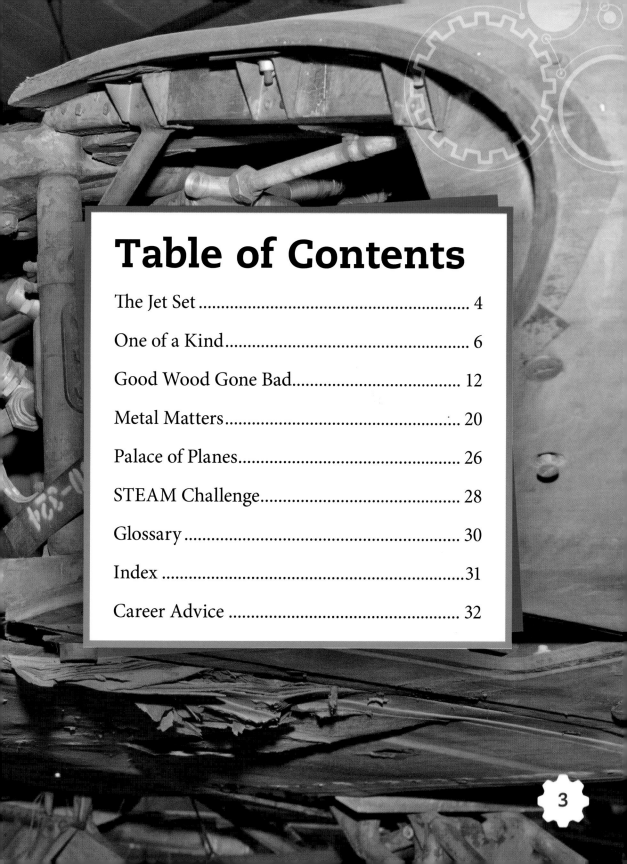

Table of Contents

The Jet Set

Some of the most incredible planes ever built sit inside a huge building near Washington, DC. The building is the Udvar-Hazy (ood-vahr-HAY-zee) Center, part of the Smithsonian National Air and Space Museum. Visitors gaze at wooden planes from the early days of flight. They walk under huge jets and get up close to small, experimental planes.

Dozens of planes hang from the ceiling. They are positioned so they seem to be flying. One plane looks out of place. It is faded and dented. The wings aren't attached. People have been fixing it for years, but the plane looks as though it was just taken out of storage.

inside the Udvar-Hazy Center

It is the Horten Ho 229 V3 (pronounced H-O-2-2-9-V-3). The Horten is the only one of its kind. It is a survivor. It has an amazing story to tell. A few years ago, this little plane was in need of care. A team of conservators at Udvar-Hazy worked very hard to save it. Conservators are people who take care of and protect old things. Their job requires a lot of science—and a lot of imagination, too.

outside the Udvar-Hazy Center

tail end of the Horten Ho 229 V3

One of a Kind

The Horten was made in Nazi Germany during World War II. Brothers Walter and Reimar (RIGH-mahr) Horten designed the plane. Germany needed a new weapon. It was losing the war. The Horten was an attempt to reverse the outcome. The plane would have been a fighter jet with incredible speed. With it, Germany would have controlled the skies of Europe.

The Horten is a type of plane designed to be all wing. This design gave it great potential as a weapon of war. But it also made the plane hard to control. The plane doesn't have a **fuselage**. That is the middle portion of a plane. It's where passengers sit or cargo is stored.

More importantly, the Horten doesn't have a tail. Planes without tails are light. They cut through the air with ease. Removing the tail makes planes faster and able to stay in flight for a longer period of time.

the Horten Ho 229 V3 in 1950

illustration of the
Horten in flight

One nickname for
the Horten is the
"Bat-Wing Ship."

sections of the Horten

The problem is that a plane's tail does a lot of important work. The part that looks like a fin and sticks up is the **vertical** stabilizer. It keeps the plane from being pushed from side to side by the wind. Flaps on the tail help the pilot steer. The two wings sticking out to the side of the tail are the **horizontal** stabilizers. They keep the plane from swinging up and down.

German engineers never figured out how to take away the tail and leave the pilot enough control over the plane. But the Horten's design came closer than any other. In one test flight, the Horten suffered severe damage when it landed. In another, the plane crashed, killing the pilot.

In 1945, American soldiers entered Germany. They captured the Horten. The body of the plane was in one town and the wings were in a different town. The U.S. military brought the plane back to the United States. Briefly, the wings were put on the body. Engineers studied the aircraft.

Then, the plane was taken apart and forgotten. For many years, it was stored outside in a crate. Rainwater got into the crate and damaged the plane.

ENGINEERING

Winging It

The Horten is a swept-wing jet. The wings come out of the body at an angle, sweeping toward the back of the plane. At high speeds, air travels over straight wings so quickly that it becomes **turbulent.** With a swept wing, air flows around the wings. Some air flows over the wing and in toward the plane's body while the rest flows along the edge of the wing toward the wingtip. This creates a smoother flight.

The Horten is an unusual plane. When the conservation team began working on it, they faced a big challenge. Normally, conservators have the original plans of a plane. They know exactly what metal or wood was used. They can even talk to people who built or flew the plane. But the Horten was built quickly during a war. All records were lost. Plus, builders of the plane were forced to **improvise**. They did not always have the materials they needed or wanted.

Before the Horten could be saved, conservators had to figure out how it was made. This information would be necessary. It would guide conservators in everything they did. It is how they would make sure they had the right tools for the job.

For eight months, the team at Udvar-Hazy studied the Horten. They talked about what had to be done. They made a plan. Then, they began to fix the plane. The Horten was challenging for another reason. Since it's the only Horten Ho 229 V3 that exists, the team did not want to change the plane too much. Instead of replacing worn-out wood and metal, they had to save it.

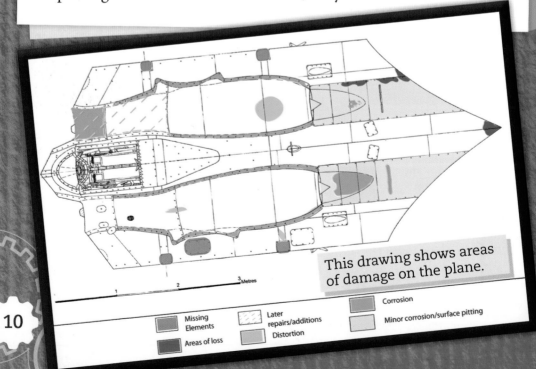

This drawing shows areas of damage on the plane.

Metres

Missing Elements

Later repairs/additions

Corrosion

Minor corrosion/surface pitting

Areas of loss

Distortion

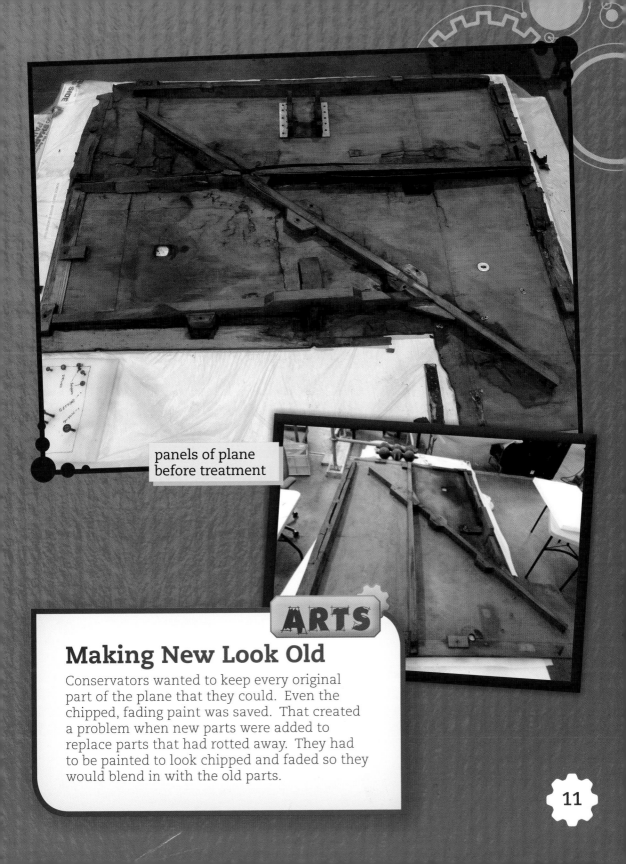

panels of plane
before treatment

ARTS

Making New Look Old

Conservators wanted to keep every original part of the plane that they could. Even the chipped, fading paint was saved. That created a problem when new parts were added to replace parts that had rotted away. They had to be painted to look chipped and faded so they would blend in with the old parts.

Good Wood Gone Bad

Most of the surface, or skin, of the Horten is made from plywood. Plywood does not grow in nature. It's made by gluing together thin layers of wood. Each layer is called a veneer.

Plywood is common—but not on planes. During World War II, most planes were made from aluminum or steel. No one knows for sure why the Horten's builders used plywood. It might have been because of wartime shortages. It might have been because the plane was experimental and plywood was good enough for a test version.

Plywood does have some advantages. The individual veneers are so thin that they can be curved. By layering veneers, builders can create complex wooden shapes.

Plywood is strong. This is because of how the veneers are layered. Wood is weakest along its grain—the wave-like lines you see in any piece of wood. In plywood, the direction of the grain **alternates** with each veneer. The grain goes up and down in one layer, then side to side in the next layer.

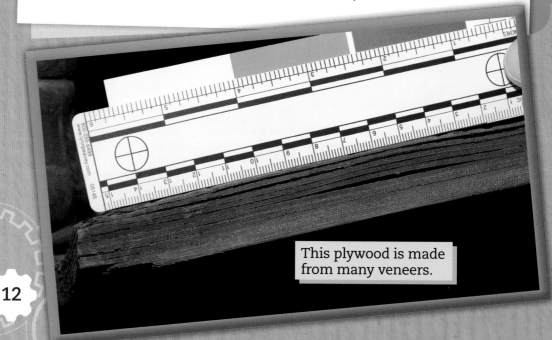

This plywood is made from many veneers.

This close-up photo shows 1.35 centimeters (0.5 inches) of plywood from the Horten.

Ancient plywood has been discovered in Egyptian tombs.

Many desks are still made with plywood.

Conservators carefully studied the Horten's plywood. What kind of tree did the thin layers come from? What kind of glue was used? How many veneers were stacked on top of each other?

They removed a tiny sample of plywood from the plane. They studied it under a powerful microscope. The layers of alternating wood were easy to see when magnified. The plywood sample showed boards made from five veneers. These boards were stacked on top of each other and were held in place by a thick layer of glue.

The conservation team needed to go even deeper to find out what type of tree the wood came from. They knew that most German plywood during the war was made from either beech or birch trees. They cut a very thin piece of wood from a single veneer. With a microscope, they looked at the structure of the wood. They found thick groups of dark-colored **cells**—a sure sign that the wood was from a beech tree. With more detective work, the team figured out the kinds of glue that were used.

Paint has chipped and faded from the body of the Horten.

cross section showing layers of paint

50 µm

MATHEMATICS

Tiny Measurements

Sometimes conservators have to measure very small things, such as layers of paint. Inches or centimeters aren't very useful at this size. Instead, microns (μm) are used. There are 1,000 microns in 1 millimeter. There are 10 millimeters in 1 centimeter. The veneers used in making the Horten are about 250 μm thick. A single human hair is about 100 μm thick.

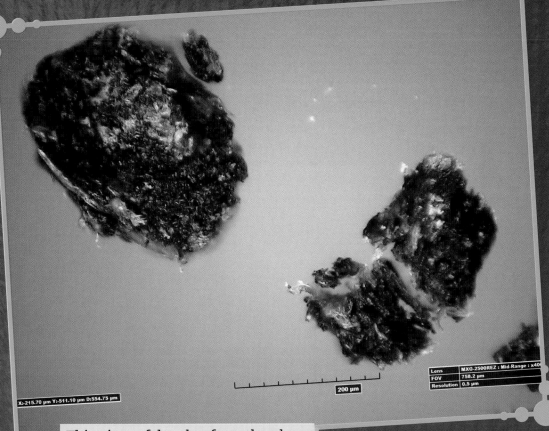

X:-215.70 μm Y:-511.10 μm D:554.75 μm

200 μm

Lens	MXG-2500REZ : Mid-Range : x400
FOV	758.2 μm
Resolution	0.5 μm

This piece of dry glue from the plane is the size of a grain of salt.

15

A top concern for the team was to save as much of the Horten's wood as possible. Under a microscope, wood looks like a handful of straws. That's because the cells that make up wood are shaped like tubes. Water and nutrients move through the tree by using these tubes.

In healthy wood, the cells have thick, strong walls. As wood gets older, the cell walls become thinner. Eventually, the cell walls are so weak that the wood crumbles away.

Conservators needed to make the cell walls thick again. They added a consolidant (kuhn-SAH-lih-duhnt). This conservation tool penetrated deep into the wood. It bonded with the cell walls. It made the walls stronger. It seemed as though the old wood was young again.

Applying the consolidant was a challenge. The team needed to be sure each layer of wood had the same amount. The layers of glue used to make the plywood gave the team another challenge. The consolidant could not pass through the glue.

The solution was very time-consuming. Using a needle, conservators injected the consolidant into each layer of the plywood.

This photograph shows a section of beech tree under a special microscope.

the tail end of
Horten Ho 229 V3

In some places, the Horten's plywood was destroyed by **fungi.** Only layers of dried, fragile glue were left behind.

After the consolidant was added, it was time to replace wood that had rotted away in big chunks. The conservation team faced another challenge. Each layer of wood required a slightly different patch. The missing wood had to be replaced one thin layer at a time.

Team members traced the shape that was missing from each board. They loaded the image into a computer. Then, they cut a matching piece with a very precise laser guided by the computer.

The team glued the new to the old—layer after layer. It was like solving the world's most complex puzzle. Most of the new wood, like the old wood, came from German beech trees. People who will take care of the plane in the future will be thankful that the wood is the same. This is because the new wood will shrink, expand, and hold paint and glue just like the old wood.

Any remaining small holes were filled with **putty** that became hard overnight. If a hole was large enough, the putty was topped with a layer of beech wood.

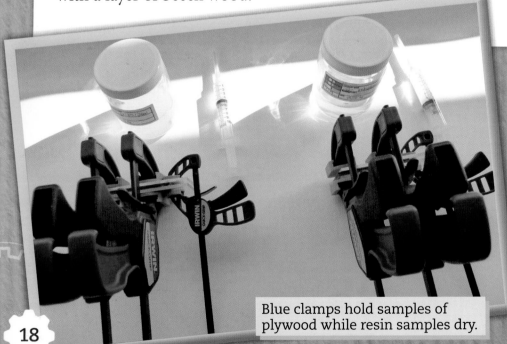

Blue clamps hold samples of plywood while resin samples dry.

A laser cutter creates closely fitting pieces for a section of the Horten Ho 229 V3.

How Do Lasers Cut?

Lasers are intense beams of light. In the case of a laser cutter, that energy is transferred to wood. It causes the wood to become so hot that it vaporizes—meaning it turns into gas. If the laser transferred less energy, it would set the wood on fire instead of vaporizing it.

Metal Matters

Even though most of the plane's skin was made from wood, areas near the engines were protected by metal. Over time, dents and scratches chipped off some of this metal's protective paint. Water found a way into these openings. The result was rust. As the rust spread, it flaked off more paint—which led to more rust.

Rust sometimes looks as though it is growing on top of metal, almost like moss on a stone. But that's not what happens. Instead, metal changes into rust. It is a chemical reaction. It's impossible to turn rust back into metal.

Fixing the Horten's metal started with a good cleaning. Conservators used a lot of the same cleaning tools people have at home. They brushed off loose rust, as well as dirt, oil, and other grime. Then, they went over the surface with a powerful vacuum. Next, they used water and special soap to wipe the plane clean.

Conservators carefully removed the thickest rust with **scalpels** and wire brushes. They applied an **acid** that keeps rust from coming back.

scalpel

A wire brush carefully removes rust from metal.

Understanding Rust

Rust is actually the result of a process called oxidation. This happens when metal is left outside in the damp air. It is a type of **corrosion.** When something corrodes, it gets weaker. Once metal changes to rust, it stays that way. The process cannot be reversed.

a heavily corroded part of the plane

before restoration

after Paraloid was applied

Plastic water bottles and LEGO®
toys are made from thermoplastics.

All the work removed the rust that was on the plane. It also stopped any more rust from forming. But there were some areas where rust had eaten through the metal. Fixing the problem required skillful fingers and some amazing technology.

The team covered small holes with a strong, thin, durable fabric. They glued the fabric in place with a product called Paraloid.

Paraloid is a thermoplastic. Thermoplastics are shape-shifters. They can change from liquid to solid and then back to liquid. They have a very important role in conservation.

There are many types of Paraloid. The kind used on the Horten is sold as small, hard pellets. When the pellets are mixed with the right chemicals, they dissolve. The result is basically plastic in liquid form. It can be painted onto a surface. When it dries, it is strong and flexible.

In the future, the conservation team might want to take off the Paraloid. Doing so is simple. With the right chemicals, it turns back into a liquid. Then, it can be wiped off.

Paraloid is applied to fabric.

The team used a similar approach in areas where the metal did not have holes but was thin and weak. Paraloid and a layer of very strong fabric were added to support the fragile metal.

In some places, rust had eaten away large amounts of metal. A different approach was needed to solve this problem. The process for filling in large gaps started with a product called Varaform. At first glance, Varaform does not seem that unusual. It is a **mesh**. It looks like something you would use for crafts. But Varaform has thermoplastic in it. When Varaform is heated, it is soft. It is shapeable. When Varaform cools, it is stiff and strong.

Conservators shaped Varaform to match areas where big metal pieces were missing. It created a base to glue fabric to. Next, Paraloid was painted onto the fabric to form a layer of plastic. Then, the plastic was painted to match the rest of the plane.

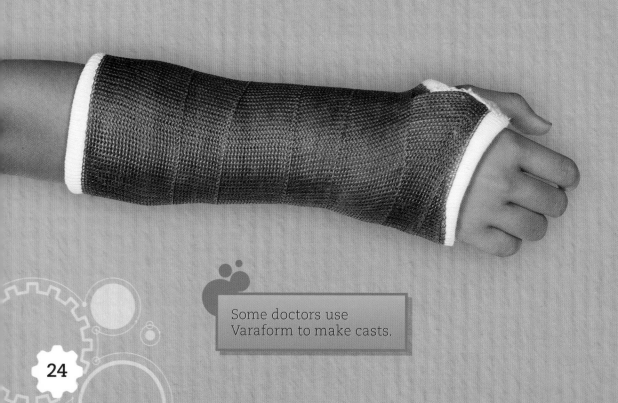

Some doctors use Varaform to make casts.

This piece of metal from the Horten has a hole in it.

Varaform has covered the hole and has been painted to match the rest of the piece.

25

Palace of Planes

Udvar-Hazy is home to more than a hundred planes. Pieces of art, engines, and even toy planes are on display. The museum even has a space shuttle and some satellites.

Each object requires the work of conservators. Their job is never done. Even when a plane is preserved, it still needs to be maintained.

The conservation team spent two years working on the Horten Ho 229 V3. In the future, they will work on the plane's wings and attach them to the body. For now, other planes need to be saved.

A million people visit Udvar-Hazy each year. They see the Horten jet as well as two gliders that were built by the Horten brothers. Visitors marvel at what the brothers made.

The work that conservators do is not as visible. There are no signs with their names on them. But **savvy** visitors know the good work they do. This palace of planes would not be possible without the conservation team.

Horten body and wings

Horten (center) along with other restoration projects

After the war, Reimar Horten built a plane that was designed to transport oranges from farms to big cities. It never made it to production.

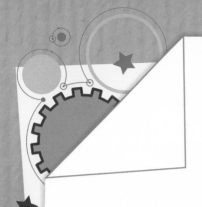

STEAM CHALLENGE

Define the Problem

The Udvar-Hazy Center gift shop wants to add a new item that visitors can buy to remember the Horten Ho 229 V3 and all the hard work done to conserve it. The gift shop manager has asked you to create a toy that is interactive. Your task is to build a replica of the Horten Ho 229 V3 that can be taken apart and put back together.

Constraints: You may not use any premade model plane parts. It must fit in a shoebox to be displayed in the shop.

Criteria: The toy replica must include all of the main design features, making it identifiable as a model of the Horten Ho 229 V3. It must be able to be taken apart into three to five parts and put back together.

Research and Brainstorm

What features does the Horten Ho 229 V3 have? What materials will you consider for your model? What parts of the plane were taken off when it was being restored?

Design and Build

Sketch your design for a new museum toy. Include measurements for each part of your model plane. Where will the plane break apart? How will the parts stay together? Build the model.

Test and Improve

Test your replica by asking someone to take it apart and put it back together. Were they able to do it? How difficult was it for them? Get feedback from your toy tester. Modify your design and test it again.

Reflect and Share

Would other types of materials provide different results? What would make the toy more user-friendly? How could you make the toy interactive in a different way? Explain your answers.

Glossary

acid—a chemical with a sour taste, such as citric acid; may be poisonous and have ability to break down materials

alternates—occurs in a series where something is done one way one time, done a different way the next time, and is repeated

bonded—connected in a strong way; connected permanently

cells—small structures that are in every living thing; the smallest units of life

consolidant—in conservation, a product that binds together loose substances

corrosion—the process of decaying or breaking down

durable—staying in good condition over a long period of time

fungi—a family of organisms that feed on organic matter

fuselage—the main body of a plane, where passengers sit

horizontal—flat; side to side

improvise—make do; figure out a creative solution

mesh—like a net; a pattern of solid areas and empty areas

pellets—small bead-like objects

putty—a soft cement

savvy—smart, aware, knowledgeable

scalpels—sharp, precise cutting tools

thermoplastic—a family of plastics that are easy to change between their hard and liquid forms

turbulent—swirling, bumpy, violent

vertical—upright; up and down

Index

Do you want to preserve old airplanes?
Here are some tips to get you started.

"Go to a yard sale or thrift store to buy some vintage items. Work with an adult to restore them using different things around your house. Keep a list of which products work best. Conservation helps you preserve a part of history." —*Russ Lee, Curator, National Air and Space Museum*

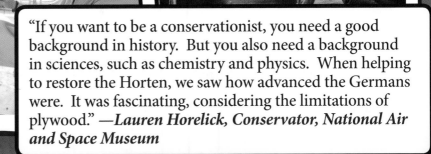

"If you want to be a conservationist, you need a good background in history. But you also need a background in sciences, such as chemistry and physics. When helping to restore the Horten, we saw how advanced the Germans were. It was fascinating, considering the limitations of plywood." —*Lauren Horelick, Conservator, National Air and Space Museum*